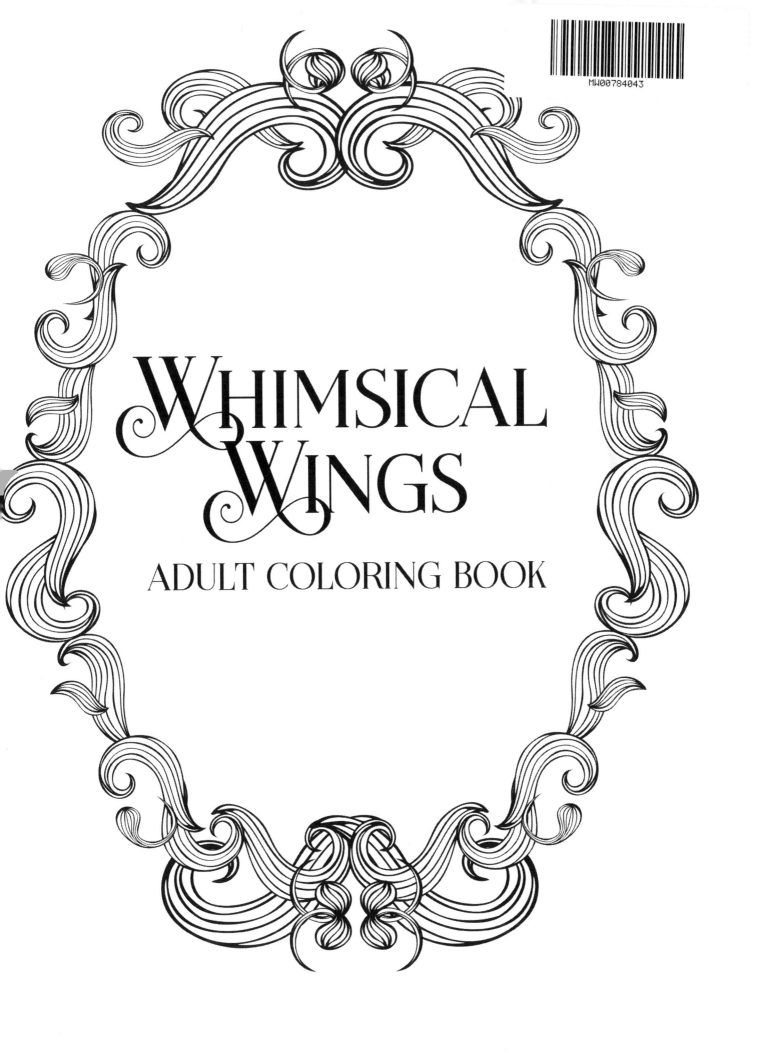

WHIMSICAL WINGS

ADULT COLORING BOOK

Whimsical Wings
Eclectic Coloring Books Vol. 3

Streetlight Graphics Publishing
For information on other books in the *Eclectic Coloring Book* Series please visit: www.StreetlightGraphicsPublishing.com

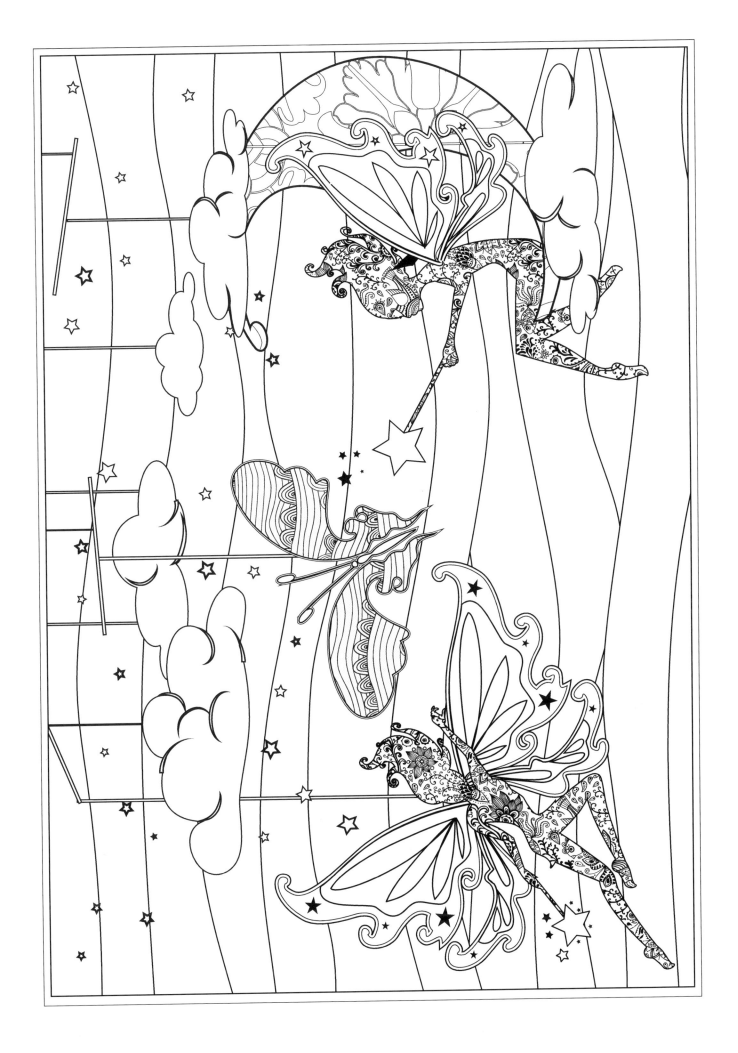

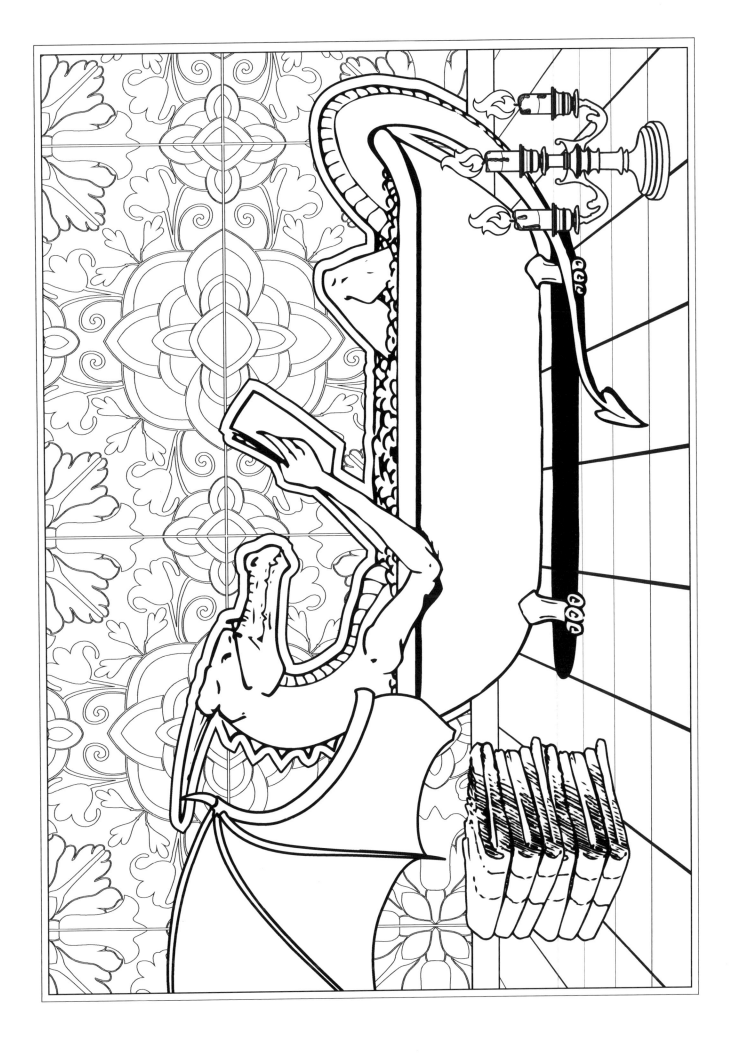

25748406R00027